My Jesus

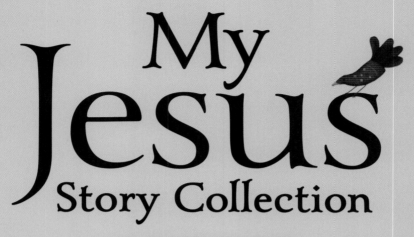

Story Collection

**18 New Testament
Bible Stories**

Retold by
Archbishop DESMOND TUTU

Edited by
Douglas C. Abrams

ZONDER**kidz**

"In the spirit of celebrating children all over the world, the artists in this book have been invited to draw on their own unique and rich cultural heritage in illustrating these biblical stories. Their art is truly a marvelous reflection of how we are all made in God's image."
—Desmond Tutu

ZONDERKIDZ

My Jesus Story Collection
Copyright text © 2010, 2019 by Desmond M. Tutu
Copyright illustrations © 2010, 2019 by Lux Verbi.BM (Pty) Ltd.

Portions of this book were previously published with the title
Children of God Storybook Bible.

Requests for information should be addressed to:
Zonderkidz, 3900 Sparks Drive SE, Grand Rapids, Michigan 49546

Hardcover ISBN 978-0-310-76932-3
Ebook ISBN 978-0-310-76933-0
Audio Download ISBN 978-0-310-76935-4

Editor: Barbara Herndon/Annette Bourland
Art direction & design: Kris Nelson/Cindy Davis

Printed in China

19 20 21 22 23 24 25 /DSC/ 15 14 13 12 11 10 9 8 7 6 5 4 3 2 1

My Dear Child,

   Do you know how much God loves you? He loves you so much, he sent his own Son, Jesus, to save you and show you the way to life. Through his actions and teachings, Jesus shows us the way to love one another. We are all brothers and sisters in God's family, and when we love our brothers and sisters the way God wants us to, we draw closer to God himself.

In this book, you'll learn more about Jesus, and you'll see that he lived and died to save all of us because he loves us with all his heart. That's what love is—it's sacrificial, selfless, and redemptive. I pray that as you read about Jesus's life and teachings, you're inspired to give like Jesus, to forgive like Jesus, and to love like Jesus.

Jesus taught us that there's awesome power in love. When we love each other the way God wants us to, we have the power to change the world. Love is the way.

God love you. God bless you.

Presiding Bishop of The Episcopal Church Michael Curry

~~~~~~~~~~~~~~~

Dear Child of God,

   The Bible says that each and every one of us—every girl and every boy— is a very special person.
   God made every one of us different—but he loves all of us equal. And no matter what happens, God will never stop loving you.
   God wants us to fill our lives with love. Jesus says we should love God, love other people, and love ourselves. How do we do this?

   By doing three important things:
      Do what is RIGHT,
            be KIND TO ONE ANOTHER,
                  and be FRIENDS WITH GOD.

God bless you,

Desmond Tutu

Jesus Goes to Jerusalem with His Parents

Luke 2

One day, when Jesus was twelve, he traveled with his family to Jerusalem to celebrate the Feast of the Passover. He was so excited that he kept asking his parents, "Are we there yet? I can't wait to see the temple again!"

When the celebration was over, the families from Jesus's village began their journey home. The children were all running and playing together along the way. Mary and Joseph thought Jesus was with his friends. But when they looked for him, he was nowhere to be found. Mary and Joseph were terribly worried!

"We must have left him behind in Jerusalem!" said Mary.

For three days they searched for Jesus in the crowded streets and markets of the city. At last, they went to the temple … and there was Jesus, sitting with the teachers, amazing them with his wisdom and how well he understood God's love.

Mary was very upset. "We have been searching for you everywhere!"

"Why were you searching for me?" Jesus replied gently. "Didn't you know that I would be in my Father's house?"

Jesus had realized that God was his true Father. Mary's eyes grew wide, and she never forgot that moment. Jesus grew into a man both strong and wise.

Dear God,
help me to speak
with your wisdom.

Jesus Is Baptized

Matthew 3 & Luke 3

Jesus's cousin John wore clothes made from camel's hair. John lived on locusts and wild honey. He was called "the Baptizer" because he was a holy man who called people to the river to wash them clean of their wrongdoing.

"God wants your hearts to be clean as well as your bodies," he told them. "Turn your cruelty into kindness, your selfishness into sharing."

"But how?" the crowd asked.

"If you have two coats, share one. If you have one loaf of bread, share half."

As he took them into the river, John said, "I baptize you with water, but someone far greater than I will come soon. He will baptize you with the fire of the Holy Spirit."

Jesus came to the river and asked to be baptized.

John said, "No, Jesus. *You* should be baptizing *me*!"

Jesus insisted, "This is God's plan."

So John led Jesus into the river and baptized him. As Jesus came out of the water, he saw the heavens open and the Holy Spirit spread its wings over him like a dove.

A voice from heaven said, "This is my beloved Son who fills me with joy."

Dear God,
give me a clean and pure heart.

Jesus in the Desert

Matthew 4

As soon as he was baptized, Jesus went into the desert for forty days to be alone with his Father and pray. He became very hungry and thirsty. The Devil came to tempt Jesus and said, "If you are God's Son, then change these stones into bread."

Then Jesus answered, "Scripture says, 'People can't live on bread alone. God's Word is even more important than food.'"

Then the Devil took him to the very top of the temple in Jerusalem. "If you are God's Son, throw yourself off the building. Doesn't Scripture say, 'God will send angels to catch you'?"

Jesus replied, "Scripture also says, 'You must not test God.'"

Then the Devil took Jesus to the top of a high mountain, looking out over all the kingdoms of the world. "I will give you power over everyone if you will bow down and worship me!" he said.

"Go away, Satan!" Jesus cried. "The earth belongs to God alone, and he is the only One who must be worshiped."

As the Devil disappeared, angels came to comfort Jesus.

Dear God,
help me to trust you when I am tempted.

Jesus Turns Water into Wine

John 2

Jesus and his disciples went to a wedding at Cana in Galilee with his mother, Mary. Everyone was having fun, but Mary noticed that the wine had run out. Afraid the party would be spoiled, she went to Jesus and whispered, "They have no more wine."

"Mother, why are you coming to me?" Jesus replied. "I am not ready yet."

But Jesus *was* ready. Mary knew it in her heart. She told the servants, "Do as he says."

Jesus pointed to six large stone jars. "Please fill them with water." The servants filled them right to the brim.

"Now," said Jesus, "fill a cup and take it to the master of the banquet to taste." So they did.

The man drank some, although he did not know where it had come from. He smacked his lips and called the bridegroom to one side. "This is the best wine I've ever tasted. Where is it from?"

The bridegroom didn't know, but Mary smiled to herself, knowing that everything Jesus gave was holy.

Jesus had turned the water into wine. This was his first miracle.

Dear God,
help me to use my gifts for your glory and honor.

Jesus Goes Fishing

Luke 5

One sunny morning, Jesus stood at the edge of Lake Galilee teaching people how they could live with joy in their hearts. As he spoke, more and more people crowded around to hear. Jesus had to step into a boat owned by Simon, the fisherman.

Jesus sat down and from there began teaching the people who had gathered on the shore.

When he finished teaching, Jesus said, "Let's go fishing."

Simon replied, "Master, we've been fishing all night and didn't catch a thing." Then he sighed. "But if you want us to try again, we will."

So they took the boat out into the deep water, and Simon and the other fishermen threw the nets into the sea. Soon they had caught so many fish that the boats almost began to sink.

Amazed, Simon fell to his knees. "Master," he said, "I am not good enough to be near you."

"Don't be afraid," Jesus said. "Follow me and you will not just catch fish, you will catch people for God."

Simon and the other fishermen left their boats on the beach and followed Jesus. They became his first disciples.

Dear God,
help me to follow you.

Jesus Teaches the Secret of Happiness

Luke 6

One day, Jesus told his followers about God's dream of a world where all the children of God are loved and cared for, and no one is left out.

Blessed are you who are poor, for all God's world is yours.
Blessed are you who are hungry, for God will feed you.
Blessed are you who are sad, for God will comfort you and you will laugh again.

Blessed are you who feed the poor, for you are the hands of God.
Blessed are you who comfort the sad, for you are the arms of God.
Blessed are you who work for peace, for you are the voice of God.
Blessed are you who are loving and kind, for you are the heart of God.

You are the light of the world. Shine! Let the world see your goodness and therefore give glory to your Father in heaven.

If you are angry with your brother or sister, speak to them from your heart and make peace. Forgive and you will be forgiven. Love your enemies and pray for them, for they, too, are children of God. Do to others as you would have them do to you. What you give to the world, so the world will give to you.

Dear God,
thank you for showing us the way to true happiness.

Jesus Blesses the Little Children

Mark 10

Jesus spent many hours teaching people about God and how he loves us all. One day, when Jesus was tired and resting, some parents arrived with their children. The children were giggling and laughing and running around making noise while their parents asked the disciples if they could speak with Jesus.

"What do you want with the Master?" asked the disciples.

"We want him to bless our children."

"The Master is resting," the disciples said. "You can't bother him now. Go home."

But Jesus heard them. "Do not chase away the children!" he called. "Let them come to me. God loves children, and when they smile, he smiles; when they laugh, he laughs; when they cry, he cries."

Jesus went to the children, and they laughed and played together for a while. He took them in his arms and hugged them. He placed his hands on their heads and blessed them. Then he told the disciples, "Everyone who wants to see God's dream come true must see with the eyes of a child."

Dear God,
help me to see your dream.

The Law of Love

Mark 12

Sometimes it seems like there are so many rules. It is often hard to know which ones are most important. In Jesus's time, people argued about which rule was most important to God.

One of the elders, bent over with age and wisdom, heard Jesus teaching his followers. The elder thought to himself, *Wow! This guy really knows what he is talking about.* The elder leaned on his cane and scratched his white hair. "You seem very wise. Tell me, what is the most important rule of all?"

"There are two," Jesus replied. "The first is to love God with all your heart, with all your soul, with all your mind, and with all your strength. The second is to love everyone as much as you love yourself."

The elder nodded. "You are right," he said. "The greatest gift we can offer God is to love him and love his children."

Dear God,
fill me with love.

The Disciples Learn to Pray

Luke 11

Jesus was praying under a fig tree. When he was done, his disciples said, "Jesus, we want to open our hearts to God like you. Please teach us how to pray."

"Praying is easy," Jesus said. "God wants to know you and bring you close. Just speak to God like a friend and he will listen. God hears your softest whisper, and even when you can't find the words, God hears what's in your heart."

"But how do we begin?" the disciples asked.

"You can start like this," said Jesus.

"Loving Father in heaven, blessed is your name.
May your dream of love and peace come true,
and may the whole world be made new.
Give us each day the food we need to live.
And help us to forgive so we may be forgiven."

Jesus continued, "What do you truly need? Ask and it will be given; search and you will find; knock and the door will open. Trust God in everything, for you are his children."

Dear God,
help me to open my heart to you.

Jesus Restores Sight and Gives Life

Mark 5, 8

A blind man felt his friends pulling him through the noisy crowd. *Is Jesus really going to be able to heal me?* he wondered. At last he heard one of his friends pleading, "Master, we beg you. Touch our friend so he can see again."

Then the blind man felt Jesus's hands gently touch his eyes.

"Can you see anything?" Jesus asked.

"I can see people, but they look like trees walking around."

So Jesus put his hands onto the man's eyes again. This time the man looked around in wonder, "Wow! Now I can see clearly!"

Another time, a man named Jairus ran to Jesus with tears streaming down his face. "Please, Master, my daughter is dying. Come quick."

When they got to Jairus's house, the girl had already died, and everyone was weeping.

"Don't cry," Jesus said. "She's just sleeping."

Jesus took Jairus and the girl's mother into the room where she lay. He took the little girl's hand and said, "Child of God, wake up!" She immediately sat up in bed!

Then her stomach growled. Jesus smiled and said, "Feed her. She's hungry."

Dear God,
thank you for healing me when I am sick.

Jesus Calms the Storm

Luke 8 & Matthew 8

Let's go to the other side of the lake," Jesus suggested one day, wanting to find a quiet place to rest. He and his disciples got into a boat and started sailing. Bright sunlight sparkled on the water, and gentle waves rocked Jesus to sleep.

But while he napped, the wind began to blow, and waves crashed onto the deck. The boat was filling with water, and the disciples were terrified it would sink.

"Master, Master!" they cried. "Wake up! We are going to drown!"

Jesus stood and spoke quietly to the wind, "Calm, be gentle." And to the waves he said, "Peace, be still."

Suddenly the wind stopped blowing, the waves stopped crashing, and all was peaceful once again.

Jesus turned to his friends, "Why were you afraid? Don't you trust God to protect you?"

The disciples stared at each other with their mouths hanging open in amazement. "Who is this man?" they whispered. "Even the wind and the waves obey him."

Dear God,
help me to trust you when I am afraid.

Jesus Is Changed on the Mountaintop

Matthew 17

Jesus said to his closest friends, Peter, James, and John, "Come with me to the mountaintop to pray."

They climbed for hours until their legs ached. At last they were at the top. Jesus's face began shining with a light as bright as the sun, and his clothes seemed to glow. Moses and Elijah, two great leaders who had died long ago, appeared next to Jesus and began to talk with him.

Peter and his friends were stunned. "Lord," Peter gasped, "we are blessed to be here. Let me build houses, and we can stay in this wonderful place forever!"

But even as he was speaking, a bright cloud came down and covered them all. A voice spoke from the cloud.

"This is my Son who fills me with joy. I love him. Listen to what he says."

Peter, James, and John covered their heads and threw themselves on the ground in fear. Jesus touched them gently on the shoulder. The cloud had gone, and Jesus was alone with them.

"We cannot stay on the mountaintop," Jesus said. "We must return to the valley where God's children need us."

Dear God,
help me to share your glory with others.

A Woman's Love for Jesus

John 12

Jesus was at the home of friends who had given a dinner in his honor. He was eating and drinking at the table and having a good time when a woman came in. She had long, black hair and was carrying a jar of precious perfume. She broke the top off the jar, and instantly the house was filled with the loveliest smell of lavender. The woman poured the perfume onto Jesus's feet and wiped them with her hair.

Some of Jesus's disciples were shocked. "What a waste!" they said. "That perfume is very expensive. She should have given it to us to sell so we could give the money to the poor."

"There will be many other times when we can help the poor," Jesus said. "This woman is preparing my body for when I die. She has done something very beautiful—she is showing me how much she loves me. What she has done today will be remembered forever."

Dear God,
let me be generous with my love.

Jesus Becomes a Servant

John 13

Jesus and the disciples gathered in Jerusalem. Their feet were dirty from walking the dusty roads telling people about God's dream. The disciples started arguing over which one of them was the greatest.

Jesus got up and tied a towel around his waist. He took a basin of water and began to wash the feet of his friends and to dry them on the towel.

Jesus's friends were shocked. "That is a servant's job!" they shouted. But Jesus quietly continued washing their feet. When it was Peter's turn, he jumped up. "Master, you will never wash my feet!"

"Then you cannot be my disciple," said Jesus.

"Lord," cried Peter, "wash my feet, my hands, my head, all of me!"

After Jesus had finished washing their feet, he took off the towel and sat down again.

"Do you understand what I have done?" he asked. "You call me Lord and Teacher, but I have washed your feet like a servant. You must follow my example. The leader is the servant of all. You must be as servants to each other. No one is more important than anyone else. I want you to love one another the way I love you."

Dear God,
help me to be a willing servant of all.

Jesus Shares His Last Meal with His Friends

Matthew 26

Jesus wanted to celebrate Passover and share a meal with his disciples so he could say good-bye. By that time, many people looked up to Jesus as a great leader. This made some of the priests and the Roman rulers very jealous. Jesus knew that they wanted to arrest him and that his life was in danger. Jesus knew it was time for him to return to his Father.

As they all sat around the table, he picked up a loaf of bread. After thanking God, Jesus broke the bread and passed a piece to each of them.

"This bread is my body," he said.

Then he took the cup of wine. Again he thanked God and passed it around to his friends.

"This is my blood," he said. "I am pouring it out for you. Whenever you break bread and drink wine like this, remember me and remember that someday God's dream—of everyone sharing and caring, loving and laughing—will come true."

Dear God,
thank you for making me part of your dream.

The Trial and Death of Jesus

Matthew 26–27

After Jesus's last supper with his disciples, they went out to the Garden of Gethsemane. Jesus stayed awake, praying alone. Suddenly, soldiers surrounded them and arrested Jesus. They accused him of trying to become king.

At his trial the Roman ruler, Pontius Pilate, asked, "Are you the king of the Jews?"

"My kingdom is not of this world," answered Jesus.

"Set him free," said Pilate. "This man has done nothing wrong."

But some people were angry. "He called himself a king," they shouted. "Crucify him!"

To please the crowd, Pilate ordered the soldiers to beat Jesus and then to kill him. They whipped him and made fun of him. Pretending he was a king, they put a crown of thorns on his head and a red cloak around him. Then they made him carry a heavy, wooden cross to a hill outside the city.

They nailed Jesus to the cross. His mother, Mary, and several other women wept at his feet and stayed with him until the very end.

Then Jesus prayed to God one last time before he died. "Father, forgive them, for they do not understand your dream."

Dear God,
help me to forgive just as Jesus forgave.

Jesus Is Alive

Luke 24 & John 20

Two days after Jesus died, Mary and several other women went to the tomb where he had been buried. They were shocked to see that the stone that had covered the opening had been rolled away. They looked inside. Jesus's body was gone! Two angels in dazzling clothes said, "Why are you looking for Jesus here? Jesus is alive! Go tell the others."

The women rushed to tell the disciples. At first, no one believed them.

A little while later, the disciples gathered to talk about what had happened. Suddenly, Jesus stood right in front of them.

"Peace be with you," Jesus said.

The disciples were so frightened they clutched each other and trembled. But Jesus said, "Don't be afraid, it is me. Look at my hands and my feet. Touch me." But they still could not believe that Jesus was alive.

"Give me a piece of fish," said Jesus. He took the fish and ate it, and his followers were convinced. Jesus really was alive and back with them again! They were so happy, they laughed and clapped their hands in joy.

Dear God,
help me to see that Jesus lives.

The Good News

Acts 1

Jesus stayed with his friends and spoke to them about all the things that had happened to him. He reminded them of the old stories, about how the prophets had promised that God would send his Son to help God's dream come true.

Jesus said, "Tell everyone everywhere that God loves them, and that those who believe in the good news of God's dream should be baptized. And in a few days you, my friends, will be baptized with the Holy Spirit."

He then stretched out his hands and blessed them, saying, "I will be with you always, to the end of time." A cloud came from heaven, and Jesus disappeared.

The disciples stared up into the sky looking for him.

Two men in white robes appeared. "Why are you looking up into heaven?" they said. "Jesus is not far away. He will always be close to you even though you cannot see him. And one day, he will return in the same way that he left you."

The disciples went home singing praises to God.

Dear God,
help me to know that Jesus is near.

Illustrators

Alik Arzoumanian
United Kingdom/United States

The Disciples Learn to Pray

Laure Fournier
France

Jesus Blesses the Little Children

Lyuba Bogan
Russia/United States

Jesus Restores Sight and Gives Life
The Trial and Death of Jesus

Jago
United Kingdom

Jesus Goes Fishing
The Good News

LeUyen Pham
Vietnam/United States

Jesus Goes to Jerusalem
 with His Parents
Jesus Turns Water into Wine

Cathy Ann Johnson
United States

Jesus Teaches the Secret of Happiness
Jesus Becomes a Servant

Peter Sutton
United Kingdom

Jesus Is Changed on the Mountaintop

E.B. Lewis
United States

Jesus Shares His Last Meal
 with His Friends

Beatriz Vidal
Argentina

Jesus Calms the Storm
Jesus Is Alive

Frank Morrison
United States

A Woman's Love for Jesus

Marijke Ten Cate
The Netherlands

Jesus Is Baptized

Stefano Vitale
Italy

Jesus in the Desert
The Law of Love